I0165960

F. W. Beers

Atlas of the Counties of Lamoille and Orleans, Vermont

F. W. Beers

Atlas of the Counties of Lamoille and Orleans, Vermont

ISBN/EAN: 9783743304536

Manufactured in Europe, USA, Canada, Australia, Japa

Cover: Foto ©Andreas Hilbeck / pixelio.de

Manufactured and distributed by brebook publishing software
(www.brebook.com)

F. W. Beers

Atlas of the Counties of Lamoille and Orleans, Vermont

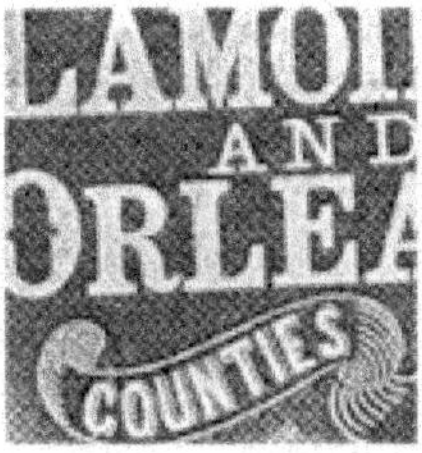
LAMOI
AND
ORLEA
COUNTIES

ATLAS

STATE HOUSE, MONTPELIER, VT.

OF THE

COUNTIES OF

LAMOILLE

AND

ORLEANS

VERMONT

Published by

F. W. BEERS & CO.

1878.

36 Vesey Street, NEW-YORK.

Entered according to Act of Congress A.D. 1878

TABLE OF CONTENTS.

LAMOILLE COUNTY.

TOWNS.

VILLAGES.

ORLEANS COUNTY.

TOWNS.

VILLAGES.

MISCELLANEOUS.

TABLE OF
AIR-LINE DISTANCES
FOR
LAMOILLE COUNTY,
Vermont.

POPULATION OF LAMOILLE COUNTY BY TOWNS.

POPULATION OF ORLEANS COUNTY BY TOWNS.

Population of Vermont by Counties.

THE UNITED STATES.

TABLE OF
AIR-LINE DISTANCES
FOR
ORLEANS COUNTY,
Vermont.

MAP OF THE
UNITED STATES

CANADA EAST

NEW YORK

STATE OF NEW YORK

FRANKLIN

ORLEANS

LAMOILLE

ESSEX

CALEDONIA

CHITTENDEN

WASHINGTON

ADDISON

ORANGE

RUTLAND

WINDSOR

NEW HAMPSHIRE

STATE OF NEW HAMPSHIRE

BENNINGTON

WINDHAM

MAP OF
VERMONT.

Scale 12 Miles to the Inch

STATE OF MASSACHUSETTS

BELVIDERE AND WATERVILLE

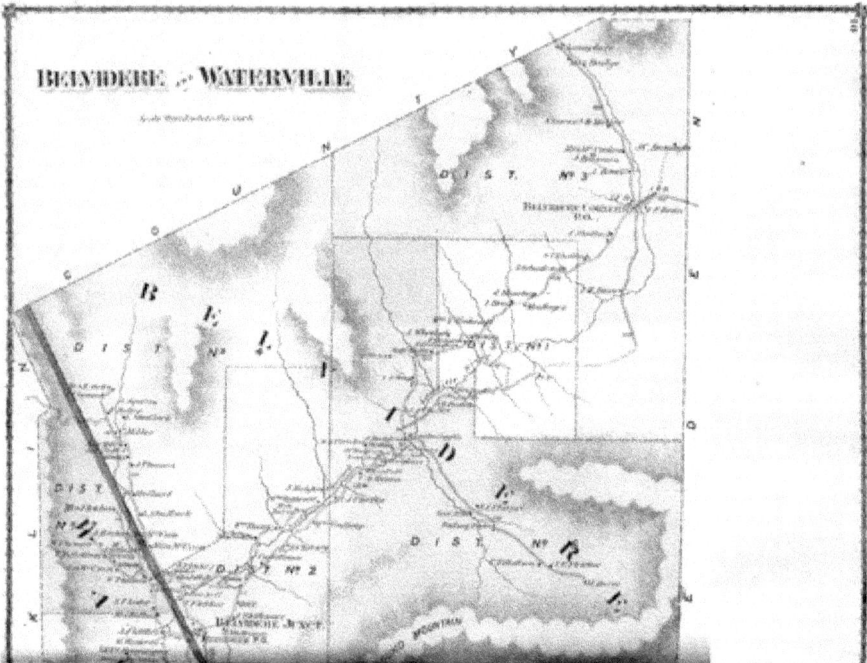

BELVIDERE JUNCTION

TOWNS OF BELVIDERE & WATERVILLE

WATERVILLE

TOWN OF WATERVILLE

EDEN

EDEN MILLS

Scale 200 Rods to the inch

BELVIDERE   EDEN

W
A
T
E
R
V
I
L
L
E

GREEN   MOUNTAINS   DIST.

N° 17

DIST.

N° 14

DIST. N° 6

DIST N° 7

DIST

J. DIST N° 10

DIST. N° 9.

DIST. N° 5

ROUND MOUNTAIN

DIST N° 11

PERKINSVILLE

JOHNSON P.O.

DIST N° 2

DIST N° 3

LAMOILLE River

DIST N° 4

DIST N° 8

STERLING MOUNTAIN

HYDE PARK

Scale two Rods to the inch

EDEN

MORRISTOWN

DIST. No 18

DIST. No 7

DIST. No 13

DIST. No 8

DIST. No 9

DIST. No 11

DIST. No 1

DIST. No 16

DIST. No 12

DIST. No 3

NORTH HYDE PARK P.O.

CENTERVILLE

HYDE PARK P.O.

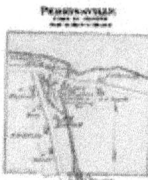

WOLCOTT

WOLCOTT
TOWN OF WOLCOTT
Scale 20 Rods to the inch

NORTH WOLCOTT
TOWN OF WOLCOTT
Scale 20 Rods to the inch

AMERICAN
BOX AND BONE CO.
TOWN OF WOLCOTT
Scale 20 Rods to the inch

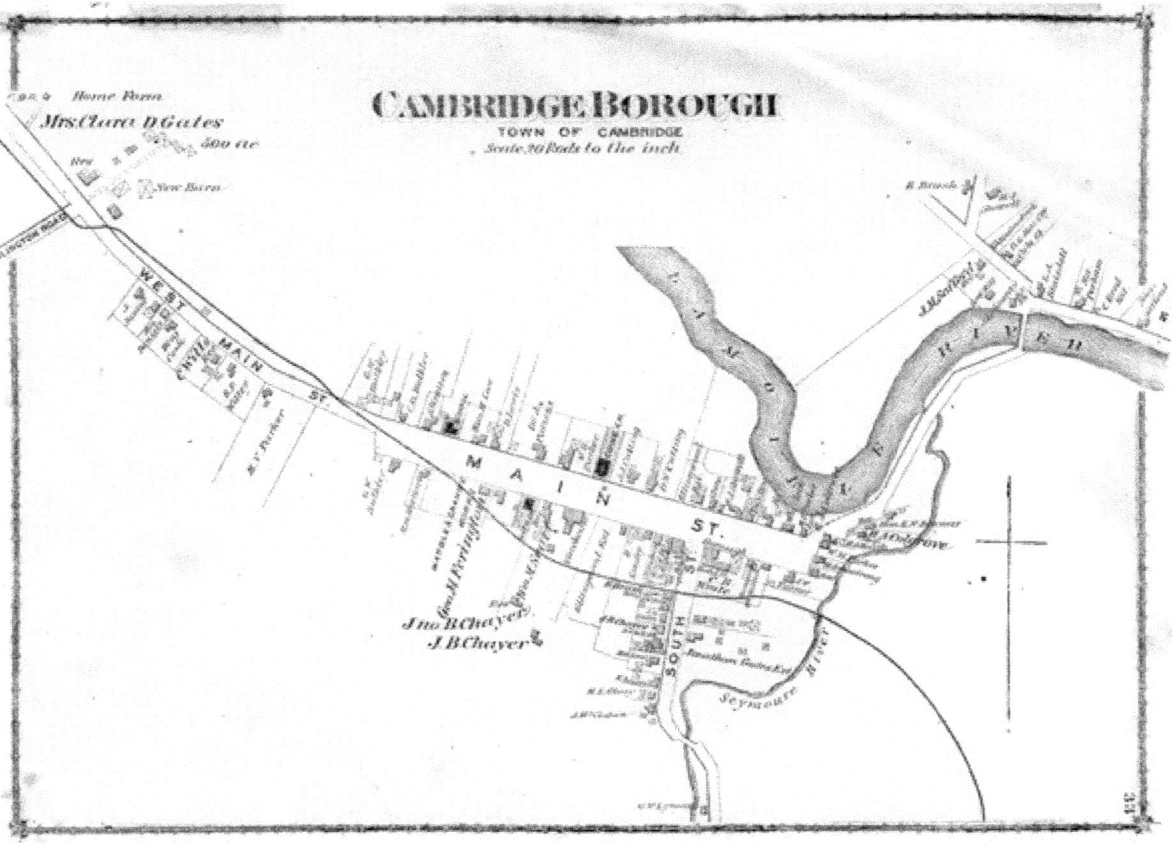
CAMBRIDGE BOROUGH
TOWN OF CAMBRIDGE
Scale 20 Rods to the inch
Home Farm
Mrs. Clara D. Gates
500 ac
New Barn
BURLINGTON ROAD
WEST MAIN ST.
MAIN ST.
SOUTH ST.
R. S. Parker
Geo. H. Perrington
Jno. B. Chayer
J. B. Chayer
J. M. Safford
R. Brush
LAMOILLE RIVER
Seymoure River

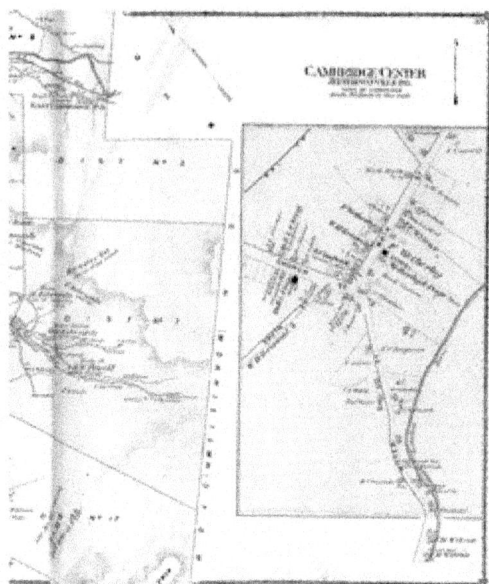

CAMBRIDGE CENTER

MORRISVILLE

TOWN OF MORRISTOWN

Scale 80 Rods to the Inch

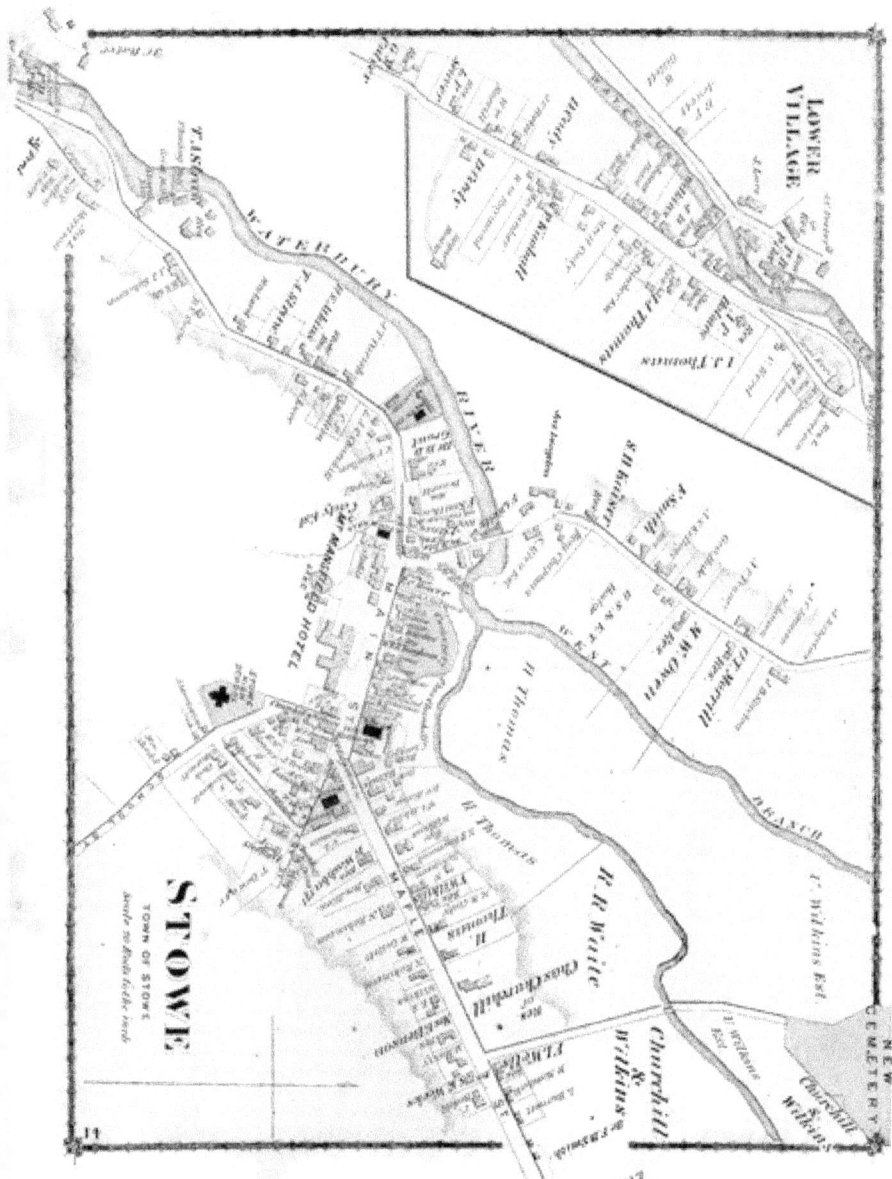

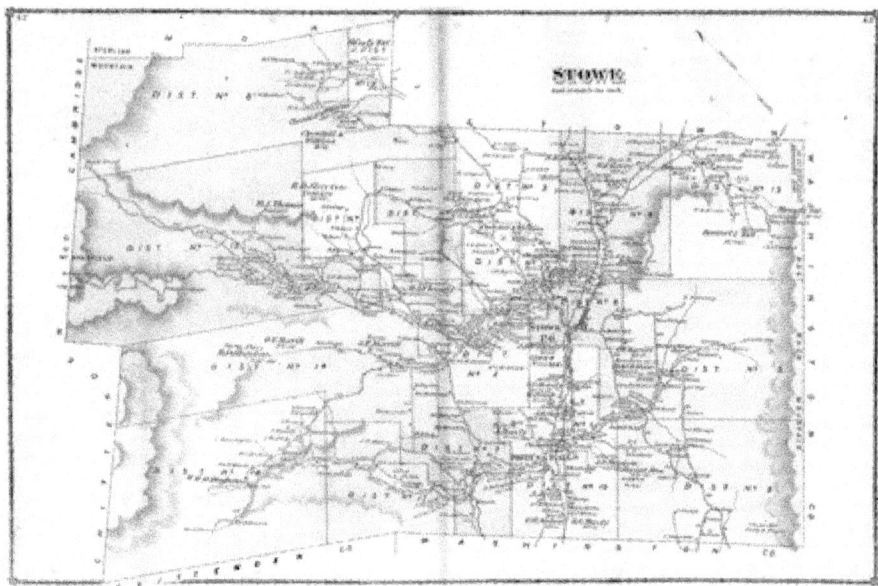
STOWE

ELMORE

Scale 100 Rods to the inch

O   L   C   O   T   T

ELMORE P.O.

Den A. Camp

D I S T   N° 3

ELMORE POND

D I S T   N° 5

SCHOOL

L. H. Doty

A. C. Merriam

A. M. Kelley

D I S T   N° 4

D I S T   N° 1

D I S T   N° 2

J. T. Parker

LITTLE POND

SCHOOL

R. F. Moore

Notch Head

EAST ELMORE P.O.

D I S T   N° 8

J. T. Hill

J. Lee

D I S T   N° 9

D I S T   N° 7

D I S T   N° 6

W   A   S   H   I   N   G   T   O   N

FRAC. DIST.

W   A   S   H   I   N   G   T   O   N   CO.

M   O   R   R   I   S   T   O   W   N

PLAN OF
ORLEANS CO.
VERMONT

Scale 3 Miles to the inch.

FRANKLIN CO.

LAMOILLE CO.

CALEDONIA CO.

ESSEX CO.

JAY

Scale 100 Rods to the Inch

C A N A D A

F R A N K L I N   C O.

D I S T   N° 6

D I S T   N° 3

D I S T   N° 4

D I S T   N° 2

D I S T   N° 5

D I S T   N° 1

JAY PEAK

MOUNTAIN HOUSE

G. W. Crandall

W E S T F I E L D

NORTH TROY

TOWN OF TROY

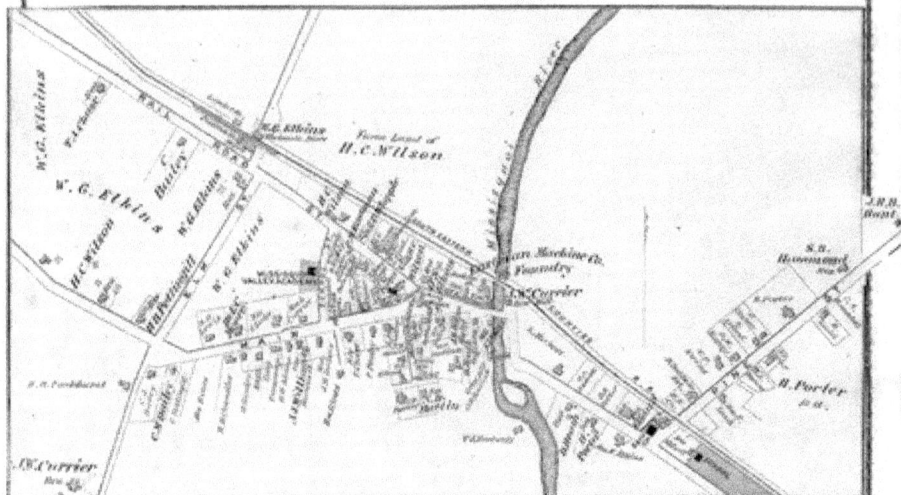

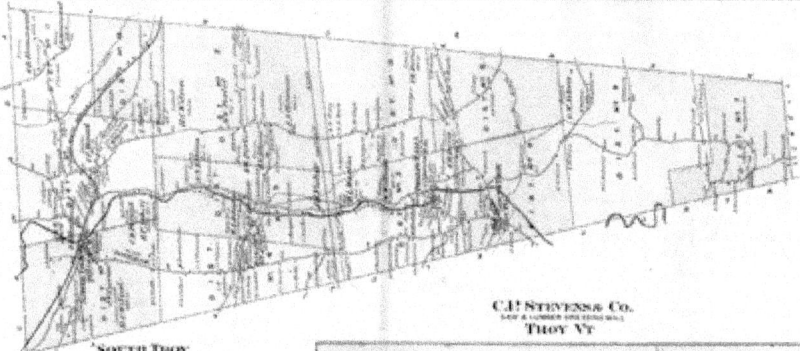

TROY

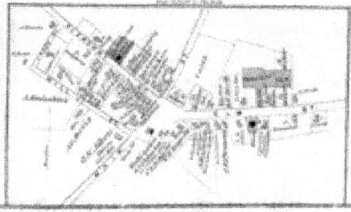

SOUTH TROY

C.J. STEVENS & Co.
SAW & LUMBER AND CORN MILL
TROY V^T

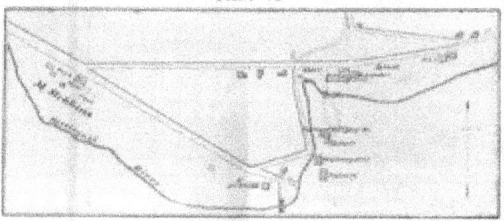

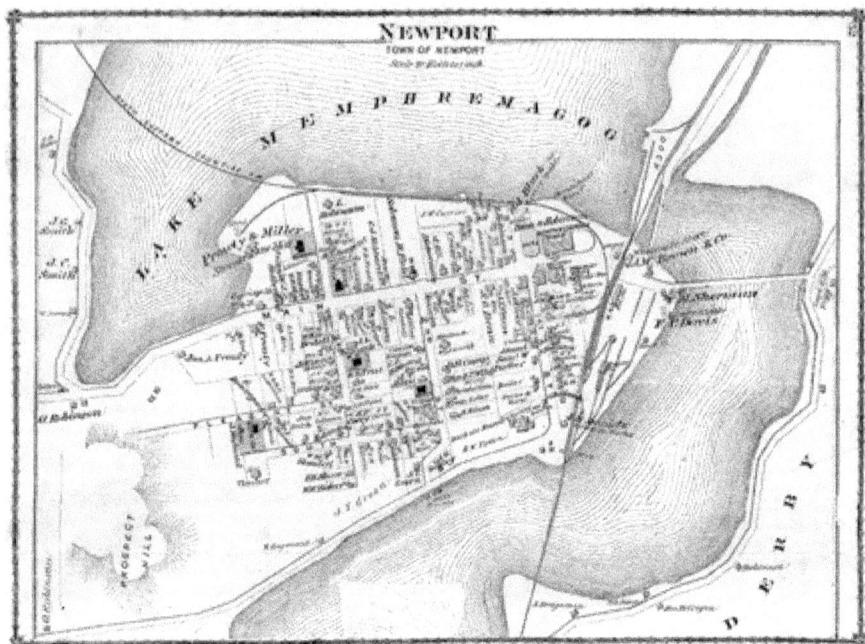

NEWPORT

TOWN OF NEWPORT

Scale by Rods to an inch

LAKE MEMPHREMAGOG

DERRY

PROSPECT HILL

DERBY

Scale 100 Rods to the Inch.

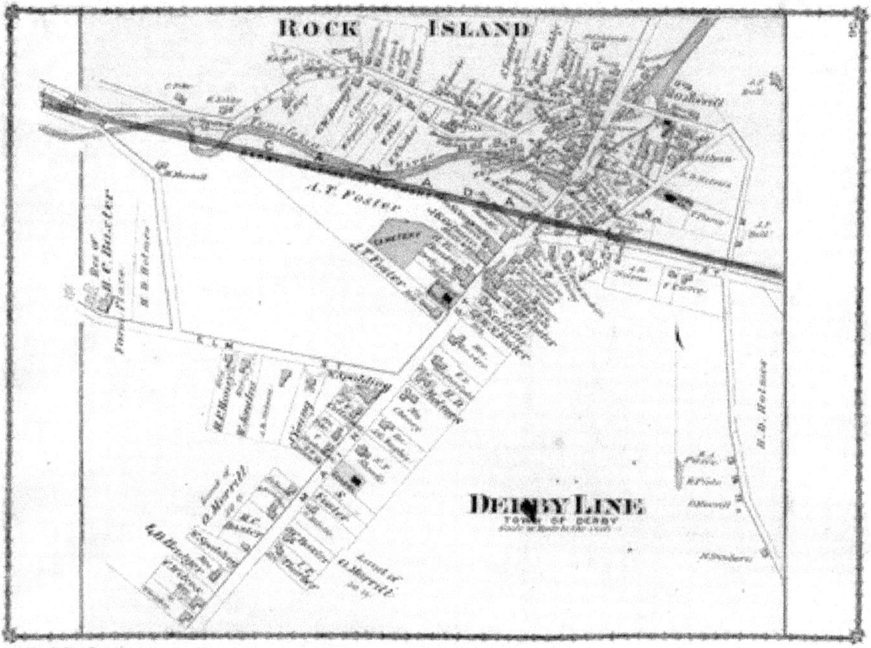

ROCK ISLAND

DERBY LINE
TOWN OF DERBY

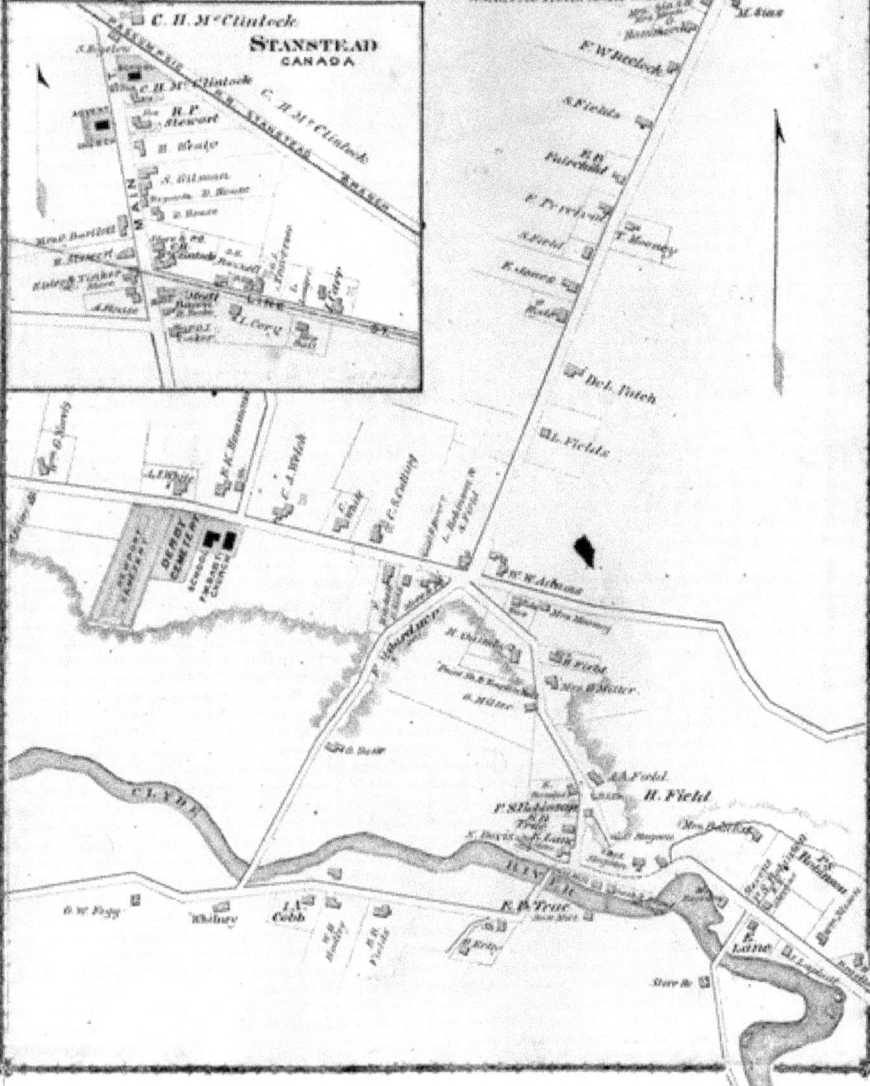

WEST DERBY
TOWN OF DERBY
Scale 20 Rods to the inch

BEEBE PLAIN
TOWN OF DERBY
Scale 20 Rods to the inch

STANSTEAD
CANADA

Durant & Adams

NEWPORT CENTER

TOWN OF NEWPORT

Scale 80 Rods to the inch

HOLLAND

C A N A D A

CANADA

DIST No 4

Holland Pond

DIST No 5

TRYPTON

HOLLAND P.O.

DIST No 6

DIST No 7

DIST No 2

DIST No 1

DIST No 3

WESTFIELD

Scale 200 Rods to the inch.

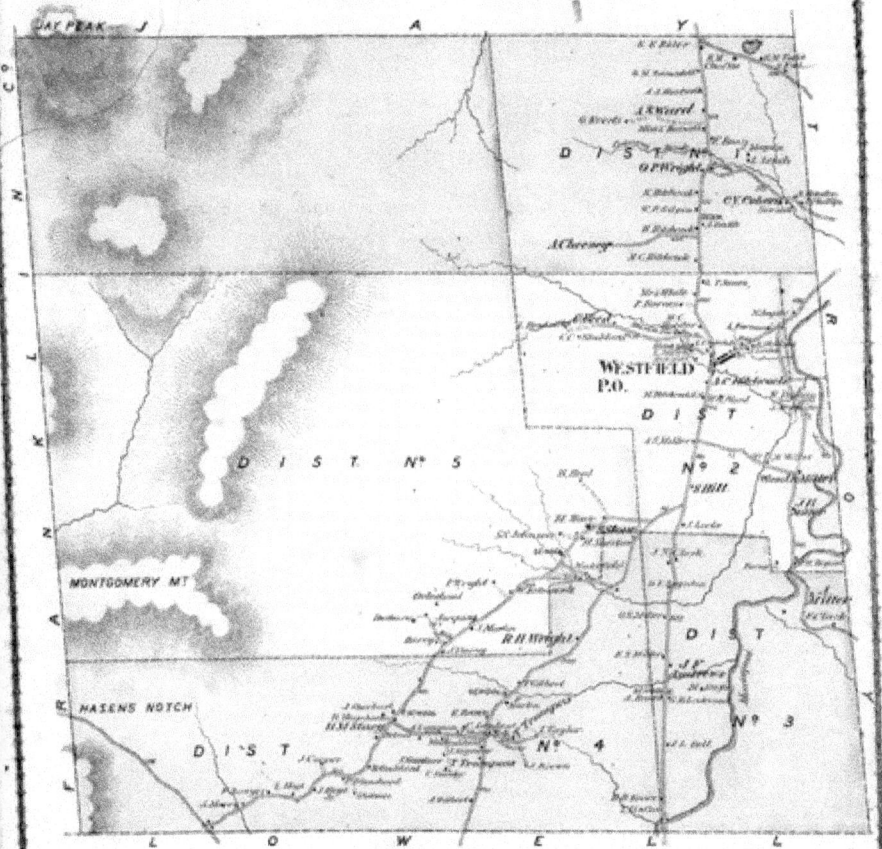

JAY PEAK

DIST N° 1

O.P.Wright

A.Cheeney

WESTFIELD
P.O.

DIST

DIST N° 5

N° 2

R.H.Wright

DIST

MONTGOMERY MT

N° 3

HASENS NOTCH

DIST

N° 4

L   O   W   E   L   L

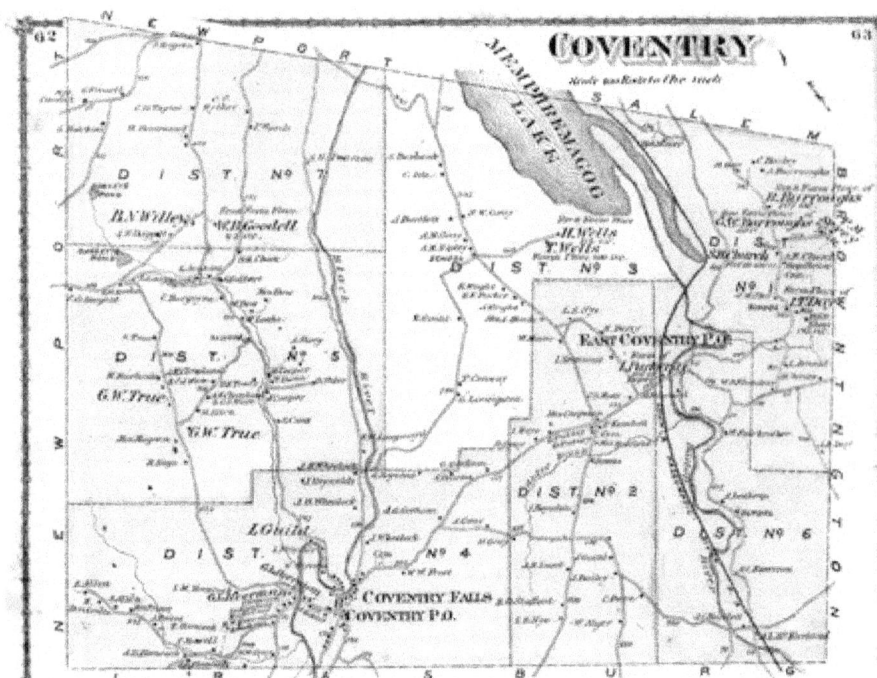

COVENTRY

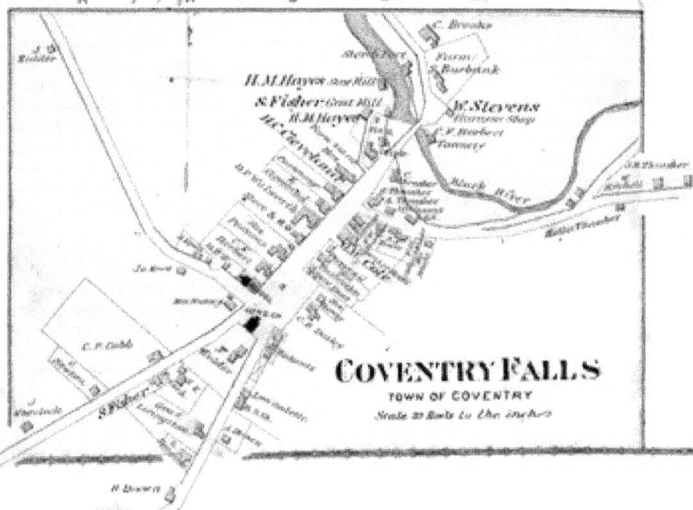

COVENTRY FALLS

TOWN OF COVENTRY

Scale 30 Rods to the inch

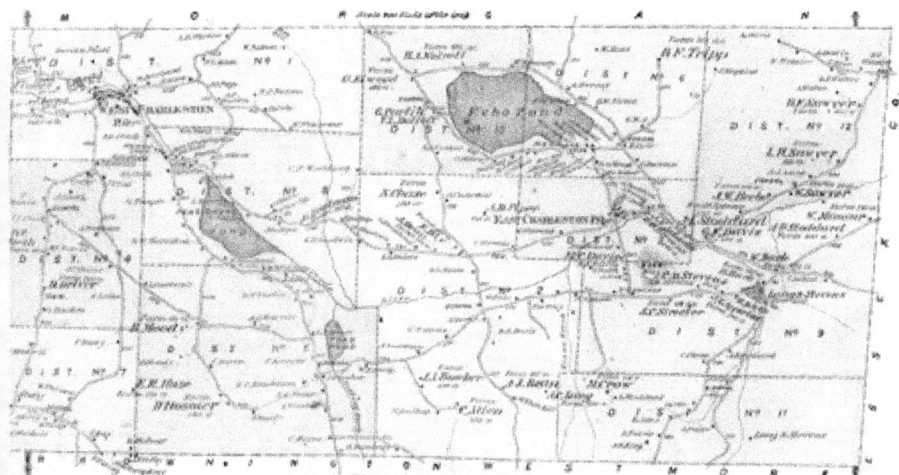

EAST CHARLESTON
TOWN OF CHARLESTON

WEST CHARLESTON

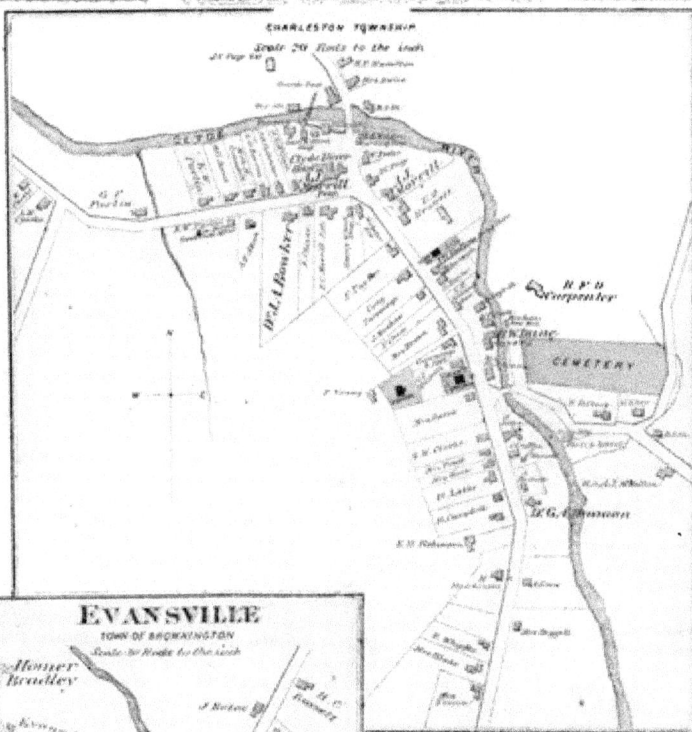

CHARLESTON TOWNSHIP
Scale 20 Rods to the inch

EVANSVILLE
TOWN OF BROWNINGTON
Scale 30 Rods to One inch

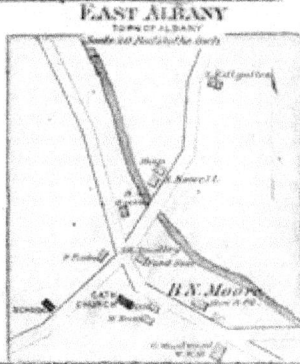

EAST ALBANY
TOWN OF ALBANY
Scale 30 Rods to the inch

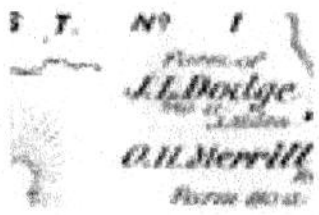

S. T. No. 1

Farm of
S. L. Dodge
the late
Ashton

O. H. Merrill
Farm No. 31

BROWNINGTON VILLAGE
TOWN OF BROWNINGTON

IRASBURG
TOWN OF IRASBURG

BROWNINGTON

Scale 200 Rods to the Inch

S A L E M

C H A R L E S T O

DIST. No 1

DIST. No 3

DIST. No 5

DIST. No 6

DIST. No 4

DIST.

DIST. No 2

DIST. No 3

DIST. No 8

BROWNINGTON VILLAGE

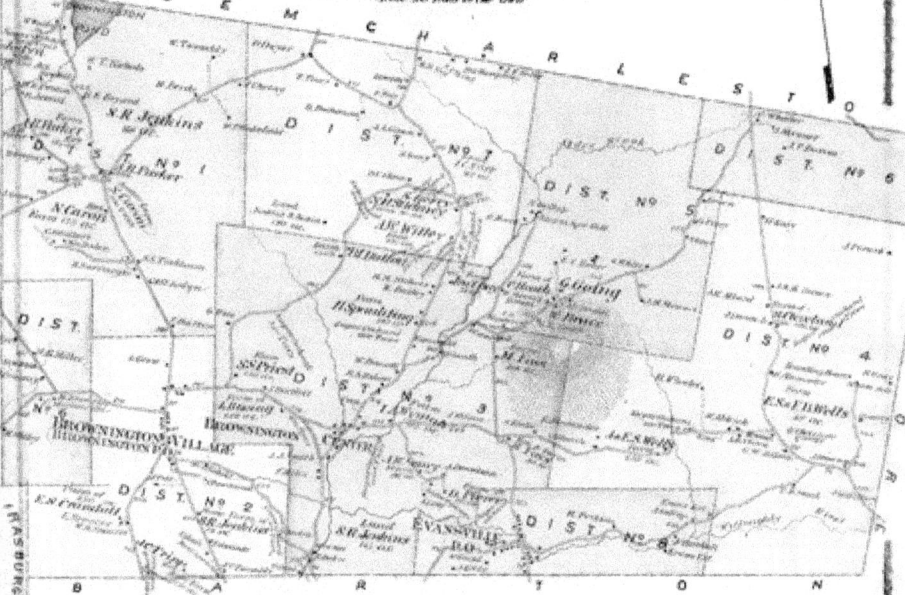

BROWNINGTON CENTER

EVANSVILLE P.O.

E R A S B U R G

B A R T O N

BROWNINGTON CENTER

TOWN OF BROWNINGTON

Scale 40 Rods to the Inch

ALBANY

Scale 100 Rods to the Inch.

WEST ALBANY
TOWN OF ALBANY

ALBANY CENTER
TOWN OF ALBANY

SOUTH ALBANY
TOWN OF ALBANY

BARTON
TOWN OF BARTON

WESTMORE

Scale two Rods to the inch

CHARLESTON   ESSEX Co.

W. Wilson   R. Marshall

J. DIST. No. 4

D.A. Haynes   James Hinton
John Hinton

BROWNINGTON

DIST. No. 2

Farm of
A.M. Litchfield

WESTMORE
P.O.

DIST No

WILLOUGHBY

DIST No. 3   LAKE   DIST. No

E.L. Carpenter
J.C. Page
E.L. Carpenter

Farm of
M.D. Scott

M.C. Blodgett

BARTON

CALEDONIA

NORTH CRAFTSBURY
TOWN OF CRAFTSBURY
Scale 20 Rods to the inch

CRAFTSBURY
TOWN OF CRAFTSBURY
Scale 20 Rods to the inch

EAST CRAFTSBURY
TOWN OF CRAFTSBURY
Scale 20 Rods to the inch

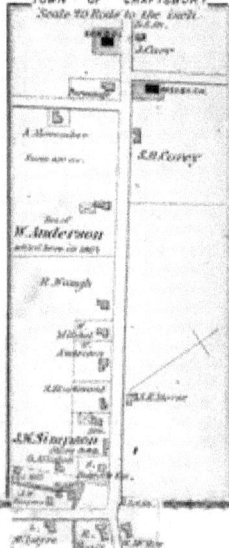

MILL VILLAGE
TOWN OF CRAFTSBURY
Scale 20 Rods to the inch

GLOVER

Scale 100 Rods to the Inch

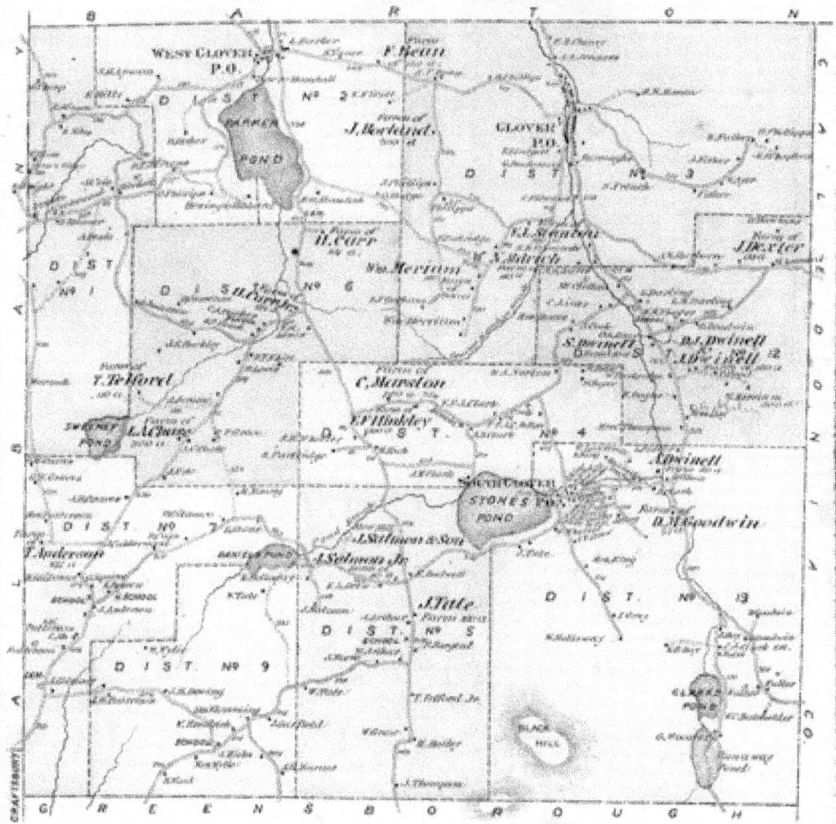

WEST GLOVER
TOWN OF GLOVER
Scale 20 Rods to the inch

H.Cutler

J.Shaw

J.W.
Fowler's

J.W.
Fowler's

R.K.Whitney

Cutler

C.Cutler

J.Spaulding

GLOVER
TOWN OF GLOVER
Scale 20 Rods to the inch

L.Bushnell

B.H.Bushnell

J.French

J.French

J.King

J.Phillips

Geo.Shaw & Co.

J.H.Drinnell

M.
Abbott

J.R.Drinnell

J.B.Chamberlain

R.L.Drinnell

Furniture Manuf.

GREENSBORO

Scale 100 Rods to the inch.

GREENSBORO
TOWN OF GREENSBORO
Scale 20 Rods to the inch

GREENSBORO BEND
TOWN OF GREENSBORO
Scale 20 Rods to the inch

LAMOILLE COUNTY

BUSINESS NOTICES.

Cambridge.

MANUFACTURERS.

GEO. H. FERINGTON, Propr. of The Cambridge Bone Harrow Works. Also Manufactured Dealer in Stoves and Scotch Granite Monuments, Tombs, Tablets, Headstones, Posts, Columns, Posts, Mantles, Shelves, Counter Tops, &c., designed and executed in the highest style of the art, from the very best Italian and Vermont Marble. Shop on State st., Cambridge Boro.

W. H. SCOTT, Manufr of Furniture and Coffins. Also Carpenter and Wheelwright

J. M. SAFFORD .... Manufr of Lumber

C. D. SAFFORD ..... Grist Mill and Wheelwright

J. M. WILSON .... Manufr of Flour and Feed

MERCHANTS and DEALERS.

C. D. GATES .... Genl Mdse

WETHERBY & PAGE, Wholesale and Retail Dealers in Dry Goods, Groceries, Boots, Shoes, Flour, Salt, and Nails, Clothing, Hats, Caps, Notions, &c., Jeffersonville

C. F. SMITH .... Genl Mdse

PHYSICIANS.

R. L. FLAGG .... Jeffersonville

C. WILLS .... Cambridge Borough

DRUGGIST.

R. SMITH, Dealer in Drugs, Medicines, Chemicals and Stationery. Family Medicines and Physicians' Prescriptions carefully compounded at all hours. North st.

POSTMASTERS.

C. F. SMITH .... Pleasant Valley

S. D. MERRIAM .... North Cambridge

JOEL M. WILCOX .... Jeffersonville

HOTELS.

R. CASEWELL .... Jeffersonville

C. B. WAITE .... Cambridge Borough

LIVERY.

C. B. WAITE .... Cambridge Borough

MISCELLANEOUS.

W. H. ARNOLD, Town Clerk, Cambridge

J. F. WILCOX, Wheelwright, Jeffersonville

W. H. HARGROVE, Blacksmith, Borough

D. KOGAGE ....

FARMERS.

JNO. BRUSH, M ....
W. F. BISHOP ....
B. W. BEAUFORD ....
S. T. BROWNSON ....
B. BARTLETT ....
F. C. CARPENTER ....
H. B. CASEY ....
J. A. CRANE ....
D. W. CHANDLER ....
T. EWE ARMY ....
R. EDWARDS ....
MARTIN ELLSWORTH ....
J. W. CAREN ....
S. W. DOWE ....
HENRY MONTAGUE ....
E. F. MUDGETT ....
B. F. NESMITH ....
C. D. MEARANS ....
H. B. NYE ....
R. PAGE ....
C. W. PAGE ....
H. G. POWELL ....
P. H. NEW ....
OTIS SEEMAN, N ....
HENRY SHELL ....
D. C. WALKER ....
GEO. H. WHITNOME ....
A. S. WATKINS ....
CHANCEY WAGNER ....
HIRAM WOOD ....
D. M. WATKINS, M ....

Eden.

MANUFACTURER.

A. & J. T. STEVENS, Extensive Lumber Dealers. Pine and Hardwood Lumber constantly on hand. Shipped to all parts of the country, at the shortest notice. P. O. address, Eden Mills, Vt.

C. A. & T. WHITE, Dealer and Manufr of Starch. Mills at Eden Mills, Vt.

MERCHANTS.

SABIN SCOTT, Dealer in Dry Goods, Groceries, Boots, Shoes, Crockery, Glassware, Farming Implements, and General Merchandise. Calf and Sheepskin bought purchasing Hardware, Eden Mills.

S. N. BURNHAM, Lumber Dealer. Plain and Matched Lumber. Also, Dealer in Dry Goods, Groceries, and General Merchandise.

HOTELS.

POND HOUSE, Eden Mills, A. Swinnell, Propr

J. HARRINGTON .... Hotel at Eden

FARMERS.

ALLEN ADAMS ....
N. A. ADAMS ....
C. A. ADAM ....
C. W. BLAKE ....
O. BAILEY ....
M. DAVIS ....
S. A. HINES ....
S. HULL ....
A. M. HUTCHINS ....
J. D. KEELEY ....
J. SCOTT ....
J. H. SMITH ....
J. J. WEST ....
J. R. WARNER ....
A. WHEELOCK ....

MECHANICS.

D. S. SCOTT, Black and Iron work done in all its branches

H. C. WOODWORTH .... General Mechanic

PHYSICIAN and SURGEON.

H. W. BACON M. D., Eden Mills, Vermont Having had quite a hospital discipline, would solicit chronic cases, wishing to cure them if possible. Will practice in Eden and Vicinity. Office open at all hours.

Elmore.

MERCHANTS.

W. S. ILLSLEY, Dealers in Dry Goods, Groceries, Boots, Shoes, Stoves, Crockery and General Merchandise.

G. A. MOORE, Postmaster. Also, Dealer in all kinds of plain and modified Lumber. East Elmore.

HOTEL.

POND HOUSE .... S. D. Double, Prop

FARMERS.

ABEL CADY ....
H. B. COOK ....
D. SAWYER ....
L. H. DOTY ....
W. H. HARRIS ....
A. T. HILL ....
A. M. KELLEY ....
HEZEKIAH LEE ....
H. C. MOORE ....
A. G. MERRIAM ....
H. N. OLMSTED ....
J. N. PARKER ....

Hyde Park.

MANUFACTURERS.

R. L. WHITNEY, Manufr of Flooring, and all kinds of dressed Lumber. Shady woods, Butter Tubs and Beans, Broom Handles, Plain and Matched Lumber. Saw and Grist Mill, Green River st.

A. NOYES .... Starch Manufr

J. F. HARRINGTON, North Hyde Park. Dealer in Dry Goods, Groceries, Hardware, Hats, Caps, Boots, Shoes, Crockery, Glassware, Family Medicines, and a full assortment of General Merchandise, offered at very low prices. Call and "C"

M. NOYES, General Merchandise. Dry Goods, Groceries and Provisions. Also, the largest Sawey Stock in Northern Vermont. All orders promptly attended to.

CARROLL S. PAGE, Dealer in Hides, Lumber and Starch. Call Skins a specialty. Parties supplied on easy terms of payment, in milling business and sales of Lumber, in satisfactory security.

BANK.

LAMOILLE CO. NATIONAL, C. S. Noyes, Prest. A. J. Noyes, Cashier.

HOTELS.

AMERICAN'S HOUSE, ... J. P. Estey, Prop. This Hotel is situated along without facilities to Johnsbury and St. Albans, on the Portland and Ogdensburgh R. R., which runs direct to the White Mountains, and connects with the Pass R. R., on the east, and St. Central on the West, making convenient stage routes, with New York Boston and Montreal. For accommodation superior is unsurpassed. Only one hotel driver to connects at Mount Mansfield, and return. Trout Fishing and Hunting, one of the chief attractions. Greyhounds while may go to healthy companion from their city Eden, are feel good accommodations for families, and a healthy climate for children.

The present proprietor having taken possession last spring has made himself quite prominent to a man who knows how to keep a hotel, and take care of his guests. Terms made very reasonable to families and pleasure seekers in general.

VALLEY HOUSE, North Hyde Park. This house is nicely located on the North Portage Road, a mile above R. R. Can not be beaten for quiet sports. Fishing and Fishing. Stock Trout in abundance. G. P. Steele, Propr.

DRUGGIST.

J. S. WHITNEY. Prescriptions carefully and accurately prepared, at the shortest notice. Laura on hand, a full line of medicines of the best manufacture. Chemical and Fluid Extracts, Fancy Soaps, Perfumes, Toilet Articles, &c. Groceries, Stoves, and the best assortment of Sugars and Tobaccos.

PHYSICIANS.

M. J. FREEMAN. Inspiration Doctor. Feels nothing of while that describes them such disease. Claims these above the crisis of men. Hundreds have been cured by him after I have received from the applicant world. Introduction to fees all diseases cured.

C. H. GROVER, ... Hyde Park Street

MISCELLANEOUS.

VAUGHN'S Self-acting Mouse Trap. Patent. This trap is always ready for business as it sets itself at once in catching a rodent, and can not get out of order. Price the best upon the market, forward of the trap, and it is ready for action. Agents wanted. N. Vaughn, Hyde Park, Vt.

A. CARTLEDGE .... Fire Insurance

Mrs. C. N. HYDE .... Residence

O. N. BAYFORD ..... Resident and Carpenter

C. A. A. ANDREWS, Painter, North H. Park

P. SAWYER .... Livery

O. A. BAYFORD, Publisher Lamoille Co. Regr.

ATTORNEYS.

WALDO DREXHAM, of the firm of Brigham & Waterman.

E. B. SAWYER ....

GEO. L. WATERMAN, of the firm of Brigham & Waterman.

FARMERS.

J. F. ALLEN ....
S. F. BARNES ....
J. O. BURGER ....
BYRON CROWFEL ....
W. B. COSSWINS ....
C. J. CROCKER ....
GEO. W. CLARK ....
IRA CONKLIN ....
C. J. DOW ....
M. J. EMERSON ....
C. F. FORD ....
F. FRENCH ....
A. M. GOODRICH ....
C. K. HILL .... Farmer and Cooper
B. HOOPER ....
J. HARVARD ....
W. D. HOLLIS ....
L. C. LAMPSON ....
H. McFARLAND ....
F. L. PEATT ....
S. G. STEARNS ....
R. A. TARBIEN ....
S. WHITCHER ....

Johnson.

MANUFACTURERS.

MERCHANTS AND DEALERS.

CARPENTERS and JOINERS.

BLACKSMITHS.

MISCELLANEOUS.

FARMERS.

Morristown.

MANUFACTURERS.

MERCHANTS and DEALERS.

ATTORNEYS.

MISCELLANEOUS.

FARMERS.

Stowe.

MANUFACTURERS.

MERCHANTS and DEALERS.

MISCELLANEOUS.

FARMERS.

Waterville.

MISCELLANEOUS.

Wolcott.

MANUFACTURERS.

MERCHANTS and DEALERS.

MISCELLANEOUS.

FARMERS.

ORLEANS COUNTY
BUSINESS NOTICES.

Albany.

MISCELLANEOUS.

FARMERS.

Barton.

MISCELLANEOUS.

MANUFACTURERS & DEALERS.

FARMERS and DAIRYMEN.

Charleston.

MANUFACTURERS

MERCHANTS and DEALERS.

ATTORNEY.

PHYSICIANS.

HOTELS.

FARMERS.

Coventry.

MANUFACTURERS.

DEALER.

HOTEL.

FARMERS.

Craftsbury.

Barton Landing.

Attorney

Insurance Agent

Merchants and Manufacturers

Brownington

Manufacturers

Farmers

South Barton.

Manufacturers

Physicians and Surgeons

Craftsbury.

BLACKSMITH.

HOTEL.

HARNESS MAKER.

JEWELER.

PHYSICIAN.

North Craftsbury

LAWYER.

MERCHANTS AND DEALERS.

RESIDENT.

East Craftsbury.

MERCHANT.

RESIDENT.

Mill Village.

DEALERS.

Derby.

MANUFACTURERS.

CARPENTERS and JOINERS.

RESIDENT.

MERCHANTS and DEALERS.

BANK.

NATIONAL BANK . . . . . . of Derby Line

ATTORNEYS.

HOTELS.

EDITOR and PRINTER.

CARPENTERS and JOINERS.

MISCELLANEOUS.

FARMERS.

Glover.

Glover.

**MERCHANTS and MANUFAC-
TURERS.**

[faded entries]

PHYSICIAN and SURGEON.

[faded entries]

West Glover.

**MERCHANTS and MANUFAC-
TURERS.**

[faded entries]

Greensboro.

FARMERS.

[faded entries]

Greensboro.

BLACKSMITH and MACHINIST.

[faded entries]

HARNESS MAKER.

[faded entries]

MERCHANTS.

[faded entries]

PAINT SHOP.

[faded entries]

SASH and BLINDS.

GREENSBORO SASH & BLIND FACTORY

[faded entries]

MISCELLANEOUS.

[faded entries]

Greensboro Bend.

MERCHANT.

[faded entries]

East Greensboro.

MERCHANT.

[faded entries]

Holland.

[faded entries]

Irasburgh.

[faded entries]

MANUFACTURERS & DEALERS.

[faded entries]

MISCELLANEOUS.

[faded entries]

FARMERS.

[faded entries]

Jay.

MANUFACTURERS.

[faded entries]

FARMERS.

[faded entries]

Lowell.

MANUFACTURERS.

[faded entries]

FARMERS.

[faded entries]

Morgan.

MANUFACTURER.

[faded entries]

DEALERS.

[faded entries]

FARMERS.

[faded entries]

Newport.

MANUFACTURERS.

MERCHANTS and DEALERS.

BANK.

ATTORNEYS.

PUBLISHERS.

INSURANCE.

HOTELS.

INSPECTOR OF CUSTOMS.

DENTISTS.

PHYSICIAN.

Newport Centre.

MANUFACTURER.

MERCHANTS and DEALERS.

MISCELLANEOUS.

DRUGGIST.

CLERGYMEN.

MISCELLANEOUS.

PRINTERS and STATIONERS.

FARMERS.

Troy.

MANUFACTURERS.

MISCELLANEOUS.

MERCHANTS and DEALERS.

ATTORNEY.

EDITOR.

PHYSICIANS.

HOTEL.

MISCELLANEOUS.

FARMERS.

Westfield.

HOTEL.

AUCTIONEER.

MISCELLANEOUS.

FARMERS.

Westmore.

HOTELS.

MILLS and MANUFACTURERS.

FARMERS.

www.ingramcontent.com/pod-product-compliance
Lightning Source LLC
Chambersburg PA
CBHW022031080426
42733CB00007B/795